The Simplicity of Faith

PART II

Detroit, Michigan
To Crookston, Minnesota

PAT BARANSKI

THE SIMPLICITY OF FAITH

ISBN (Paperback): 979-8-89672-259-5
ISBN (Hardback): 979-8-89672-261-8
ISBN (Ebook): 979-8-89672-260-1

PROMINENT
BOOKS
EDGE

5830 E 2nd St, Ste 7000 #9983
Casper, WY 82609
USA

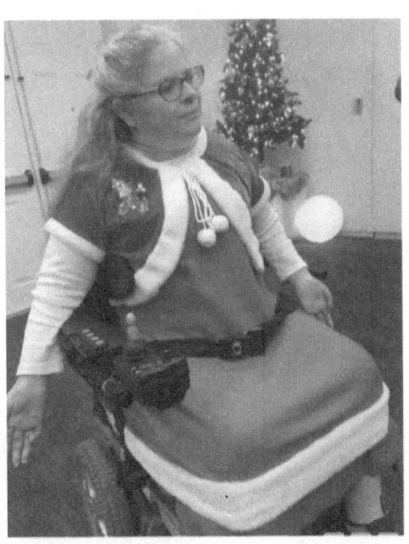

In Loving Memory of Mickey
A Dedication to Our Daughter—A Life Well-Lived

This book is lovingly dedicated to our daughter, Mickey—who is now with God, resting in His eternal peace. Her life remains a radiant reflection of God's grace, courage, and unwavering faith.

For 36 years, Mickey lived as a quadriplegic, yet her life was never defined by limitation. Instead, she shone brightly as an example of resilience and devotion. Her strength was not merely physical—it was spiritual, rooted deeply in her love for the Lord and her faithful walk with Him.

From a young age, Mickey accepted Jesus Christ as her Savior. Her heart belonged wholly to God, and she spent her life joyfully serving others through Him. Whether helping to organize Sunday School, Vacation Bible School, or other ministries within the church, Mickey gave of herself with compassion, energy, and purpose. Her dedication touched lives far and wide—and continues to do so.

Through every trial, she taught us what it truly means to live with grace and intention. She reminded us that faith triumphs over fear, that love is stronger than pain, and that a life anchored in Christ is a life of eternal value.

We honor Mickey not only as our beloved daughter, but as a faithful servant whose legacy of love and light lives on in every heart she touches. Though her earthly journey has ended, her story continues in the lives she changed—and in the glory of God's presence, where she now abides.

With immeasurable love and admiration,
Her Father, Rev. Pat Baranski

Dedication to Our Son, Glen

With deep gratitude, I dedicate this message to my son, Glen.
Your generous heart and steady support—especially with emails, computer work, and all the behind-the-scenes help—have been a true blessing.

Your willingness to step in, assist, and guide me through unfamiliar tasks has meant more than words can express.

Thank you for always being there when I needed you most.

With love and appreciation,
Your Father, Rev. Pat Baranski

With Heartfelt Gratitude to the Team at Independence Plus Inc.

I wish to express my deepest appreciation to the dedicated team at Independence Plus Inc.

Your kindness, patience, and unwavering support have been a continual source of strength and encouragement throughout this journey. Whether offering a helping hand, sharing your expertise, or simply being there when it mattered most—your contributions have left a lasting and meaningful impact.

Thank you for standing beside us, for believing in the mission, and for helping carry the vision forward.

Your partnership has made a real difference, and I am truly grateful.

With sincere thanks,
Rev. Pat Baranski

This book is dedicated to those who may be reading it out of curiosity, wondering why someone would write a book about himself. Well, it's not. It is about what God did to me and through me because I put Him in first place.

The memories I have may be different from other family members and friends because of the age difference and perspective of growing up unwanted or in the way.

Acknowledgments

THIS IS MY STORY OF how God had a plan for me through many years of good and bad religious experiences to personally see myself as lost and in need of a Savior.

There are many people who helped to bring me to the point of knowing my need and lost condition:

The girl who sat in the desk in front of me when we moved from inner-city Detroit to Dearborn Township, Michigan, and her faithfulness in prayer.

My loving, patient wife, and a pastor in Goose Creek, South Carolina, who counseled my wife and prayed for my salvation also.

They were faithful in prayer, eight years after the finger in my face. My wife and children were with me on that Sunday morning.

The conviction started in the church parking lot with the greeter shaking my hand and saying, "Good morning. Aren't you glad you're not in jail?" I thought to myself, *Oh no, he must have known me when I was in the Heights Men.*

The Reverend Robert Porter, the pastor at the time, who gave the altar call at the end of his message. I responded, and as I started down the aisle, I thought the lady across the aisle was that girl who sat in front of me eight years ago and told me she would pray for my salvation.

I was too ashamed of myself for the way I treated her, I didn't want her to see my face.

I walked down the aisle to receive Jesus Christ as my only Lord and Savior, freeing me from the sins that bound and held me captive to a materialistic world.

I raised the right side of my coat so that girl from Haston school would not see how ashamed I was because of the way I treated her eight years before.

The Neumanns, Morgans, Halls, Dows, Angers, Greens, Warrens, Dehls, and many others who prayed for us and gave us wise counsel. May God bless you; and by God's grace, we'll meet again here, there, or in the air.

The Reasons for Writing This Book

IN A WORLD GROWING MORE wicked and politically correct by the minute, someone needs to speak up and say the truth and tell what life was like before political correctness replaced common sense.

The prophet Jeremiah said, "O LORD, I know the way of man is not in himself; It is not in man who walks to direct his own steps" (Jer. 10:23 NKJV). God has a plan for everyone. It's just that people have other things that dominate their lives.

> For I know the thoughts that I think toward you, says the Lord, thoughts of peace and not of evil, to give you a future and a hope. Then you will call upon Me and go and pray to Me, and I will listen to you. And you will seek Me and find Me, when you search for Me with all your heart. I will be found by you. (Jer. 29:11-14a)

What is first place in your life?

To say that the past two generations lack common sense does not address the failures of their materialistic parents and the failing school system. I am thankful to the Lord for His Word. His Word was being taught to me by my father. He was careful not to tell me within hearing distance of my mother where he was getting it from to avoid conflict with her. He would say, "This is what my father taught me. If you want a good life, do what I tell you, and you will have a good life."

Because of the prejudice during and after World War II, my father did not tell me that the principles he was teaching me were coming from the Jewish temple my grandfather went to on Saturdays after they moved from Pennsylvania to a city that had a Jewish synagogue. At a family reunion in July 2019, my cousin told me that his father (my dad's brother) also attended the Jewish synagogue on the east side of Detroit. My grandfather had passed on before I was born, but the stories of his moonshine business lived on for years.

My father was not always the perfect example in everything he did.

Drinking moonshine during his teenage years gave him health problems for years. However, the medical problems he had were not understood by me as a kid. My father did not get treated for them until he had to have his digestive system treated because of the alcohol he started consuming at a young age. My mother told me about his prostate cancer and aneurysm shortly before he died.

The family, including my father and grandfather, were members of the local Catholic church on the east side of Detroit. My father never said his dad went to that church.

A book titled *Business Proverbs* contains much of what my father was teaching me: sound biblical principles.

Knowing who to believe and what to believe in would come in a later date.

The old saying "Actions speak louder than words" is true, as the actions of my father toward the priests (at Saint Bridgett's) showed that he was not in agreement with them or the way the church did things. That I would learn when I was to be confirmed.

This book covers the period of my life from my birth in Detroit, Michigan, to our departure from Westland, Michigan, to the village of Casco, Wisconsin, and our move to Watertown, Wisconsin. The second half of this book will cover the years after.

Someone reading this will say, "What is the point of reading this?"

The point is that God's Word stands true and that He has a plan for each of us.

I was taught biblical principles by my father at a very young age. However, there is a promise by King Solomon in Proverbs 22:6: "Train up a child in the way he should go. And when he is old he will not depart from it." My father would say, "Do right because it is right," which I'll address in more detail. I was being taught that.

You're more likely to see people in need, sometimes just holding a door for a lady or someone with their hands full or greeting someone with a warm smile.

It was not till years after both my parents had passed on that I found out my grandfather was Jewish and many other family members who were also Jewish. Only once did my father tell me that his father went to the synagogue or sought the rabbis for guidance. Years later, while in Israel, through a source there, I found out there were two rabbis with the same last name in the temple in Jerusalem.

Putting this altogether didn't come until about four years ago, when a professor was giving his testimony about seeing what another prisoner had written on the ceiling of the prison above his bunk.

> For I know the thoughts that I think toward you, says the LORD, thoughts of peace and not of evil, to give you a future and a hope. Then you will call upon Me and go and pray to Me, and I will listen to you. And you will seek Me and find Me, when you search for Me with all your heart. I will be found by you, says the LORD. (Jer. 29:11-14a NKJV)

Through all the near-death situations I had survived and the people who crossed my path and guided me in the right direction and said they would pray for me, I am truly thankful. Putting all of the story together didn't start till eight years after both my parents had passed on.

Chapter 1

MY BEGINNING

IN OCTOBER OF 1946, ON a Sunday morning at Mount Carmel Hospital, in Detroit, Michigan, I came into the world.

My father's intoxicated celebration was for a weekend or two according to my mother's complaints as she told me when I was old enough to know what a drunken celebration was.

Years later, my father explained to me the story behind his celebration.

The reason for the move from their home near Rouge Park to inner-city Detroit.

My father was concerned about a part-time deputy sheriff getting overly friendly with my mother. The man was caught by my dad with his arm around my mother's back. This part-time deputy was also a part-time electrician. Because of this situation, my father had gotten a loan from my mother's stepfather to buy the house in inner-city Detroit on Tuller Street. To my understanding, the agreement allowed my father to work off the loan, which is what he did, on weekends and some of his vacation days.

Weekends were always fun in the summer, as we would go to Orchard Lake.

As my father worked off the loan from my mother's stepfather, we would spend the weekends and holidays my dad had off from his regular job at Ford Motor Company in Dearborn on the far west side of Detroit. The farm was located west of Tipton in a community like none other I have ever been to.

A Close Farming Community

Looking back, I can picture the progress of farming from horses and mules to an army jeep and to a real farm tractor. The community of farmers did farming together. They started with spring plowing and tilling, planting, harvest, and storage. They ate lunch at whichever farm they were working at hat day. I know that when they were at my grandfather's. One of my chores was to set the cables for thirty-six farmers at lunchtime in the large dining room or outside.

A Compassionate, Caring Community

The closeness of this community was closer than many families are in the current generation. There was a situation where the parents of a young teenage girl had died in a car accident and sickness. The grandparents raised her. The grandfather was dying, and the grand-mother was sick and not expected to survive much longer.

There were a lot of tears, but in front of the community of farm families, she gave her granddaughter to a neighbor. Do you trust your neighbors that much?

I spent a lot of time with animals. They had quite a variety: mules, horses, rabbits, chickens, ducks, geese, cows, dogs, cats, and pigeons living in the hayloft.

I was given chores to do in the kitchen and the big dining room or outside if it was my grandparents' turn to feed the neighborhood crew. I had to set the tables for thirty-six as that was how large the neighborhood crew was.

My grandparents and Uncle Frank taught me how to milk the cows that they couldn't use the milking machine on. Being as young as I was, if Uncle Frank caught me playing with the kittens when I was supposed to be milking the cow next to him, he would aim the cow's tit at me and squirt milk in my face. He was teaching me to stay focused on the job at hand, rather than the kittens.

One time I was out in the barn in the milking parlor by myself, playing with the kittens and watching them as they ate. I made up a story about a monster in the barn and told it to my grandmother. She said I was quite the storyteller as she related my monster story to my mother.

I really liked feeding the kittens and calves. I liked watching the pigeons until Grandma wanted to eat the pigeons and had Uncle Frank wring their necks.

Several years later, they had to put down much of the herd because of the cows testing positive for TB from the droppings of the pigeons in the hayloft. By then my dad's loan was worked off.

Years later, shortly before getting out of the navy, I was given a blood test and found to be a TB carrier. God's protection was there even though I didn't know it (Ps. 146:9).

Chapter 2

THE CONNECTION
TO THE FARM

The Story Behind the Intoxicated Celebrations

I WAS ABOUT TEN OR twelve when my father started to explain to me why there was a big gap in age between me and my siblings.

The problem started long before I was in the picture. My father was spending a lot of time at taverns and pool tables. My mother made some connection with a part-time deputy sheriff/ electrician, which developed into a longtime affair.

All the things that happened from then till years after their move from the home they lived in, by Rouge Park, had to do with that. When my father confronted my mother after years of drunken arguments, he told me that he told her she had to give him a son before she could be reconciled with him. That was the story behind the twelve-year age difference between me and my youngest sister, the loan, the move, and the working on the farm.

My father explained to me how much my mother's affair had hurt him. The affair continued after they moved. One of the workers who worked with my dad told him he had seen the electrician's work truck near our home on Tuller. My dad said he was probably doing some wiring. His buddy said, "He was probably wiring your wife." The drunken arguments continued until my father caught the deputy sheriff/ electrician with his arm around my mother's back. He said he could arrest my father for threatening a law officer. There were two other stories of them being seen in bed together. After many arguments, my mother agreed to stop taking birth control and have a son by my father. Reluctantly my mother complied. My mother didn't want any more children after my two sisters and a brother. She agreed to give him a son.

Twelve years after my younger sister was born, I was born.

There were other things that were going on in our home while living in inner-city Detroit.

Because my father has such a large family, many of whom were living in Pennsylvania, I would be left at my first cousins who lived on the east side of Detroit. When their parents were going to Pennsylvania and we were not, they would leave their kids with my family. Because of the closeness of age with my cousins, we had more things in common than I had with my sisters and brother.

My Grandfather's Brother

My grandfather's brother who had lived in Pennsylvania and retired from the Pennsylvania Railroad lived with us on Tuller. The story about Uncle Tony that was told to me was that when he was very young, he fell out of the high chair and injured his back. His injury made him hunchbacked for the rest of his life. He stood about five feet tall at best. He could outrun me for short distances till I started gang fight training with the Tuller gang.

Uncle Tony had a few strange things about him. He came and lived with us, in the basement, on the other side of the piano. The first very stinky memory of Uncle Tony was he would come up from the basement, sometimes in his long underwear, and fix his breakfast in a small pot, big enough for a large cup of coffee, a full slice of bread, two raw eggs, and topped off with Limburger cheese. Once the bread was mushy, he would stir it; and the smell would empty out the kitchen, except for him. He made funny noises as he ate it.

The second thing was watching kids hit their heads. When he saw younger kids who were old enough to understand money, he would place a coin six inches from a wall and tell one of them they could have it if they could pick it up with their mouth with their hands behind their back. He laughed as they hit their heads on the wall or their noses on the floor.

The third crazy thing was along this same crazy way of thinking, he would get the attention of a group of youngsters and throw a handful of change, just to laugh at them hitting their heads on one another.

The fourth crazy thing that got him moved to the nursing home was going through everything he could get into when we were not at home and putting peanuts with shells in the pockets of the clothes hanging in the closet. That did it for my parents. They put him in a nursing home. Months later, he hung himself in the shower at the nursing home.

Chapter 3

LITTLE THINGS THAT MATTERED TO ME

ABOUT THE AGE OF EIGHT years old, three little things happened that impacted my life.

The first was the teaching of what is now called business proverbs. What my father taught were mainly from the Old Testament, Psalms and Proverbs, which is different, as a book titled *Business Proverbs* includes both New Testament and Old Testament business proverbs. He never said where they were coming from other than "This is what my father taught me. If you want a good life follow my instructions."

> Do whatever you do so well, people will pay you to do
> it again. (Eccles. 9: 10a)

Applying the first little thing that my father taught me was how to catch night crawlers and dig for worms. The community was in need for a bait business. We had one neighbor who lived in a triplex next door to us, who loved her lawn, and a few others who let me catch night crawlers on their property. We had two sportsmen with boats who wanted night crawlers and worms and paid me well for them. At one point, my father asked me how many night crawlers and worms I had underneath the back porch. I went under the porch and counted them (it took me a while, because I couldn't count very fast). I told my father I had five hundred night crawlers. That worked out well along with cutting lawns, raking leaves, and shoveling snow for these same neighbors.

To go along with the jobs and bait business, he taught me to be honest—use what you have wisely, and be a good steward of what you have. If you don't have the money to pay cash, keep saving till you do. At fourteen, I opened a savings account. By sixteen, I started paying cash for whatever I needed. I didn't know how to write a check till after we were married a year.

The second little thing happened when I was about eight years old. A kid about twelve years old came to the backyard dressed as a Cherokee Indian. He was part Cherokee and said he would teach me how to be an Indian. He taught me where to get the wood to make a bow and arrows, how to harden the tips, and how to shoot. This fit together well for one of the next major changes in my life. Because of his presentation and knowledge of Native Americans, he also taught me how to be an Indian: making and shooting a bow and arrows was a real good start on what was going to happen in the future.

I did not have a prejudice against Indians. I later married one.

He, however, went from playing with toy cowboys and Indians to a fascination with organized crime such as Al Capone and the Purple Gang. In his late teens to early twenties, he organized his own drug and prostitution business. I can't verify that, but that's what I was told by those who stayed in the area.

My mother was not overjoyed in having a little boy to take care of. I was often pawned off on my younger sister, who is twelve years older than me. This worked out until my sisters started dating. My brother was in school sports, at work, or in college; so he was not around most nights.

The Ice-cream Shop Abduction

The Ice-cream Shop was styled like what we would now call a Dairy Queen. It was also located in the Jewish part of town on the next block, which had an impact on my life. I was abducted by a Jewish woman. She was not mean to me. She just grabbed me by my shirt on the shoulder and said, "Little boy, you're coming with me." She took me across Fullerton Avenue and North for two or three houses. She told me she would pay me a dollar to help her clean her house, because her family was coming for the weekend. I didn't resent her for what she had done, as I had always gotten along with the Jewish people on the next block.

She taught me how to clean her house, behind the furniture, dust, vacuum, pick up clothes, and help her with whatever she needed. I did the best I could. Whenever I went to the ice cream store, I would see her looking for me again. That worked out well for everything you could buy for a dollar back then.

> Whatever your hand finds to do, do it with your might. (Eccles. 9: 10a)

Injury #1: An Injury That Changed My Social Life

My mother would reluctantly get me up for school and get me dressed and out of the house so she could go back to sleep.

I was dressed and out the door running down the alley sliding on the long sheets of ice from the wagons and trucks. I knew I was running late, but I couldn't pass this long wide one. I stopped, went back, got a good running start, and, about two-thirds of the way, fell. I used my hands to keep my face off the ice. There was something sharp sticking up that gashed my left hand. I went home bleeding and woke my mother up, and she took me to the doctor to get stitched up. My mother didn't want me continuing to interfere with her social life. I did not understand at the time why my mother was trying to convince the doctor to give me a diagnosis of attention deficit and oppositional defiant so she could put me in a group home. The doctor didn't go along with it.

Every major injury I had in my childhood made a major change in my social life.

My injury and healing time changed my activities, and in doing that, I made a new friend. George got me interested in Indian guides and helped me get a job at the same time I was supposed to be at confirmation classes on Saturday mornings, which I didn't like going to anyway. His father sponsored me after many warnings by my strongly Catholic relatives that they might present something that was not acceptable by my mother or our Catholic relatives.

Learning how to be an Indian came easy. What I had learned from the older Indian down the block was a real good start. Hiking and going swimming at the boys' club and YMCA and doing things with the Boy Scouts were very good social changes for me, for the present and more so for the future.

However, this job and dropping out of confirmation classes put me behind on being confirmed when my mother's relatives and Saint Bridgett's had planned for it.

I went back to classes. I didn't like having my ears and hair pulled or being punched in the arm. I was confirmed. It didn't make me a better Catholic, just a confirmed one.

That was the last major hurt while living in inner-city Detroit, Michigan.

My mother could no longer have someone else take care of me, as my sisters were dating, and my brother was away at college. I didn't understand it at the time, but it was resentment that I was interfering with her social life. As time went by, she would take me with her. She would tell me to play with the neighbors' kids or sleep in the back of the car if it wasn't too cold or in my aunt's bedroom if it was.

Chapter 4

THE NEIGHBORHOOD

ACCODING TO MY BROTHER, THE neighborhood we moved into from living on Warwick Street by Rouge Park was nice. My mother dressed me like a mobster's kid in a three-piece suit till third grade. By the time I was old enough to play with other kids in the community, the neighborhood was no longer the way my brother remembered it (that was sixteen years earlier). Then my brother remembered Detroit.

At the time I was living in Detroit, there were still cultural neighborhoods.

Ours was strongly German. We were Polish, but Catholic, so we got a pass from most Germans. Helen, a nice Jewish girl who lived up the block on the other side of Buenavista, was not treated as an equal by a number of the German families. One block over was a Jewish neighborhood. Helen would have been treated as an equal there. I was always treated well by the Jewish people and the British folks on that block. I was often sent to Hilands' to buy challah bread that my mother called Polish egg twist.

I started kindergarten at Noble Elementary School, which was one of the first schools in Michigan to have racial problems that made the national news. The truth is many children of different races from Fort Wayne had been coming to Noble Elementary School for many years. It was when the neighborhoods around Noble Elementary School began having racial changes that people started to protest at the school. I had friends of other colors and races who moved into the neighborhoods or came from Fort Wayne.

I Got in Trouble

There is something about me that has gotten me in trouble many times: "blatant honesty." About third grade, a new kid came into my class. He was from the Dominican Republic. He liked to bully me, punch me, and make fun of me, because I was short.

I drew his name for a Christmas present. I did not want to give him anything or have my mother give him anything. I found some old fountain pens, wrapped them in some old purple tin foil, put his name on it, and took it to school. Of course the teacher wanted to know what the new kid got; he showed the teacher. The teacher wanted to know who drew his name and asked who had his name.

Being honest, I answered her, "Me!" The teacher asked me why. I told her, "Why should I give him anything when he likes to beat me up?" She called my mother and sent me to the office.

There were a number of older kids who had fathers or a grandparent who had been POWs during WWI or WWII and had shared their memories of the war. So the older Tuller gang members tortured and sexually abused the younger kids of the neighborhood. One time I saw one of these gang members coming after me on a bike. I started to run across the street and was hit by a car. The driver stopped, but not in time. I was hit in the knee. The older kid rode away. I cleaned it and put a bandage on it, once it stopped bleeding.

Gang Training

As I got older, the older gang members started me on gang fight training: throwing rocks and green apples, making wammows, and learning how to shoot them. We also learned how to jump from garage to garage. We were having gang fights with the Turner gang quite often; I was hit with rocks and apples, shot with wammow bands, and hit with a pellet gun. Luckily it was not a straight-on shot, as it bounced off a garbage can and got me in the side of the head.

About this time, my younger sister was getting more serious about her dating.

My dad informed me that when I turned eighteen, my stuff and I would be on the other side of the doorstep on the front porch. However, he said he would teach me how to make it on my own if I followed his instructions.

The instructions were taught on weekends when he wasn't working on the farm. He was teaching me more hands on, how to do maintenance work: doors, windows, toilets, roofs, and gutters, and using basic hand tools.

He told me to be careful who I loan my stuff to. He then told me a story about the kid next door to their house on Plumber Street, in his old neighborhood. The kid next door borrowed his wagon, went to the railroad tracks, broke the government seal on the door of the boxcar, and stole a large can of lard. It had just started to snow before he loaded the lard in the wagon. The railroad police followed the wheel tracks to his house where he unloaded it then continued to my grandparents' house to return the wagon. Once there he crossed the yard, climbed the fence, and went home. The police followed the tracks of the wagon.

My father got sent to Reform School. While there, the warden taught him to fix his breakfast and how he wanted it fixed: eggs over easy, bacon crisp, but not burned. My father taught me how to do this and had me practice cooking it for him, to check my progress. It was one of the things I impressed the regular cooks with. It was one of the other jobs I did when the cooks found out I could cook in Fort Knox, Kentucky.

Over the next five years, my father taught me maintenance skills that paid off in the following fifty-four years. His instructions helped me to set up three profitable businesses, learn a skill trade, plus serve in a variety of jobs in the military for over twenty-eight years.

Don't Pass Up Free Money

When my mother figured I was old enough to be left at home by myself, I would sit by the upstairs window and watch the happenings of the community: I took note of the times of police patrols and the actions of the women living in the triplex next door. Often the women would give the cabdriver a tip of a coin, and he would grumble and throw it. I would silently watch where it landed and go out and pick it up after she went in and he drove away. It wasn't much, but two or three times a week, it made it worth the time of watching and waiting.

During this same period, we were still driving between Detroit and Tipton, Michigan, so my father could pay off his loan to my mother's stepfather.

I was old enough to start noticing what my mother was doing. I asked her about embroidery. She showed me how to do it. As time went by, she taught me how to iron and use a roller press, replace buttons and zippers, and tailor clothes. I found out later in life that I had six uncles who were tailors. The training paid off well, while I lived in Fort Knox, Kentucky. I did tailoring, pressing clothes, shoe and boot shining, and a couple of other jobs while being at basic training for the Michigan National Guard.

While still living in inner-city Detroit, my mother thought she had found the ideal girl for me. The girl was from the other side of the tracks and a student at Saint Bridgett's Catholic School. She had also stabbed me in the chest with an old-fashioned fountain pen, because I had teased her while she was babysitting. Six years later, she inquired about me at the bakery where my wife worked at.

About the time we moved from Detroit, older members of the Tuller gang were robbing businesses and breaking into homes. At one point, one of the gang members whose father was a cop broke into a government warehouse, took a swing at the guard, and was thrown. When he hit the ground, he rolled and ran off before the guard could catch him. That was enough for me. I was watching from a distance and didn't want any part of that.

Chapter 5

THE MOVE FROM INNER-CITY DETROIT TO DEARBORN TOWNSHIP

WE MOVED TO A CLOSER location to our relatives, a smaller house with a bigger yard, bigger garage, fruit trees, and grapevines. It was also closer for my father's job and my mother's sisters. We were almost on the border road next to Dearborn. Only five blocks from the local school, four blocks from what would become the city hall. The township became Dearborn Heights, shortly after our move.

When I started school, the girl with the long blonde hair I mentioned who sat in front of me started praying for me. I got into sports—soccer and track.

Injury #2

I got two paper routes. I managed to cut my hand on the bottom of the seat of my bike as I was on my way home, so I stopped at the fire department to ask for a bandage. They rushed me off to the ER. To get stitches, I got it stitched up, and my mother came and got me.

Injury #3

About the time I was getting good at soccer, I got hurt again. This time it was a big deal. Both my lower leg muscles were cut. I had over two hundred and fifty stitches between the two legs. I had trouble walking. Once I could walk, I started sparring to practice my foot-work in boxing. I sparred with an older gang member. I started going hunting and purchased a twelve-gauge double-barrel shotgun.

Injury #4

The gang got me involved in various unlawful things that I wasn't comfortable doing on my own. I got in a fight with a gang member that left me with bruised ribs, a broken nose, and a broken collar-bone. Last I heard, he got kicked out of the military and went to prison. That was pretty much it for injuries for me for about two and a half years. Until I was in the navy, in Norfolk. I was in a fight with three guys. I was winning until I was thrown down the steel steps. I got knocked out but was okay when I woke up.

Back to Gang Life

I had to steal a car to prove I could do it. I did it, drove around, let them off about nine blocks from where I had taken it, and took the car back from where I had taken it. (It was my boss's car. He never knew I took it.) They stopped bugging me about not knowing how to steal a car.

The local gang took the name the Heights Men. I joined the gang but never got my gang colors. At about this time, my father didn't like the late-night card games and the guys I was running with. My mother was very much a part of many of the card games. My father continually told me I would be known by the company I kept.

As time went by, I got more into sports, working, and hunting.

Shortly before I turned sixteen, my mother was changing the sheets on my bed and lifted the mattress and found an empty whiskey pint bottle and a twelve-gauge shotgun between the mattress and box springs.

My mother went to Dad and said, "You deal with him."

My father told me I had to take the gun back. He would get me a gun when he felt I was ready. There was little to nothing said about the empty whiskey bottle.

The Story Behind the "No Guns Near Your Mother"

He then told me why he didn't allow guns like that anywhere near my mother. Then he explained to me how my mother acquired a shotgun.

My mother had gotten a twelve-gauge double-barrel shotgun that had been involved in a shooting. A couple had been in an argument. She grabbed the gun my mother now had. She threatened to shoot him. He turned around, pointed his butt at her, and said, "Go ahead, shoot!" She did. My father had a fairly new car, and Mom and Dad went out by the landfill to shoot pigeons. My mother took the loaded shotgun. Standing by the car, she pulled both triggers, putting a big dent in the car door. The deputies nearby came and took the gun they had been looking for from the shooting.

My father said I had to learn gun safety before I could have a gun. He drove me there the first time, to the Ford Gun Club to learn gun safety. The following eight weeks, I rode my bike there and back. Sixteen miles round trip.

Shortly before my twelfth birthday, my folks had bought a cabin north of Hale, Michigan, a mile south of the dance/pool hall, where I would meet my future wife.

When I was between the ages of twelve and fifteen, my father would do repair jobs for my uncle on his lake homes at North Lake and at my cousin's buildings east of Barton City.

While working with my father, my uncle was under the house trying to level it from sliding down the hill toward the lake. My uncle was way under the house, near the middle of the house. My father and I were on the south side outside the crawl space. I watched him hold the jack in place to stop the house from shifting on my uncle while he was being stung in the face and neck by hornets. My uncle got out, and they stabilized the house and came back with bug spray.

For a number of years, my father did repairs on my cousin's property just outside of Barton City, which had been a large chicken operation.

I had some good friends in the Barton City area and over by the reservation. After I had my driver's license, my cousin paid me to drive his vehicle and trailer from Dearborn to Barton City, but I had to take his younger brother with me.

How to Pick a Wife

About this time after we came back in the city, my father gave me the "how to pick a wife" lecture. My mother was in the next room, so she could hear him. He said, "First off, don't get one like your mother." She went off. He said, "Don't pay any attention to her. Listen to me." His instructions included domination of in-laws. His instructions helped me pick my wife of over fifty-four years. God had a plan. I didn't know it.

Change of Diet

The beginning of a diet of pizza and beer.

With my father working afternoons, my mother having her own social life, it did not leave a lot of leftovers out. My mother made it clear to me: "Be home by midnight and don't come home drunk." When I came home drunk, my mother would hit me over the head with a frying pan. She gave the frying pan to my wife. My wife asked me why it was so rounded in the center. I told her it was from beating me in the head when I came home drunk.

I was working, and Larose's Pizza was only four lots away, and it was easy to buy beer, even though I was underage. One large meat pizza and a six-pack was a daily diet for me, unless I was with my folks.

Pressure to Leave

I was in the Heights Men. It was humiliating to have a police car waiting at my house when I was walking home with the neighbor girl. Whenever the gang committed a crime, the police were waiting at my house when I was on my way home from school. I would be questioned and released, after the school would verify that I had been there when the crime had been committed by the gang.

I quit school, got a second job, and worked out an agreement with my father, that if he signed for me to go in the U.S. Navy, I would finish school before I got out of the navy.

I went to the testing room for the test to join the U.S. Navy. I fell asleep before I finished it and failed. I was bummed.

I spoke with a Michigan National Guard recruiter. He explained to me how I could give the guard a try and then transfer to the navy if I wanted to.

I filled out the paperwork, took the test, passed it, and got a better job. The job worked out well. I got a promotion, and I was approached to consider management training for what would become Kmart.

I was sworn into the Michigan National Guard two weeks before President Kennedy was assassinated. I wanted to leave for basic training as soon as possible.

I took on another part-time job I could work before I went to my main job.

Months went by. I was going to the drills and training for field communications.

I spent much of my Sunday evening / Monday morning losing my whole check playing cards, my mother being one of the players.

I said to myself, *You're being stupid. Go back to school.* It was Monday morning. I was changing clothes. I just put a clean shirt on, when the phone rang telling me I was leaving for Fort Knox, Kentucky, in two days. What a time to be in Fort Knox, Kentucky.

Chapter 6

THE DEPARTURE FROM MICHIGAN

I DEPARTED FROM DEARBORN HEIGHTS, Michigan, after two days of goodbyes and best wishes. The train station had a number of crying families for their sons who had gotten their draft notice.

I took a two-day train ride to Louisville, Kentucky, then a bus ride to Fort Knox for in-processing into the army basic training.

It took me about two weeks to figure out how the military system worked. When I realized how many draftees did not know how to do the simple things that I had been taught as a teenager by my father, I was able to set up a business shining shoes and boots, pressing clothes, doing clothing repairs and alterations, and cooking.

I had mess cooking twice before the cooks found out I knew how to cook. It started with breakfast then went on to the other meals. I checked the schedule to see what I didn't want to do and checked the mess cook duty list. I approached whoever was on the list and told them my price for taking their mess cook duties. They paid me. I cooked.

I made a profitable business out of what my mother and father had taught me. I made it through basic training and into on-the-job training in field communications as a lineman crew member. I had no problem or fear of heights after jumping from garage to garage or jumping off the second-story roof of the Detroit Public Works in Detroit.

I was in Fort Knox at a very interesting time with the Combined Forces' Presentations and the filming of *Goldfinger* and the Kentucky Derby going on in June and July of 1964. That was the first time I was around that many state and federal representatives at the same time.

Two of the Same

Shortly before my training was nearing completion, I realized that there were two of us in the same unit who looked alike. Though different in age by five years, he looked younger, and I looked older. We even had the same blood type. I could wear his uniform. I just had to memorize his service number. He was going to Vietnam upon completion of training, and he had to see his girlfriend back in Columbus, Ohio. So, for a generous sum of money, I became him for a three-day Fourth of July weekend that included military police duty. He made it back on time. I went back to Michigan the following week.

Chapter 7

RETURN TO MICHIGAN

I HAD ENOUGH MONEY SAVED that I didn't have to work between my release from active duty in Kentucky from the Army National Guard to going on active duty in the U.S. Navy.

In August, I went to the pool hall / dance hall, north of Hale, and found the girl who would become my wife in January of 1965.

On our second date, I proposed to her. She said she was engaged to a fella in the army, serving in Germany. I found out where she lived and went in to speak with her stepfather about why I was a better choice for a husband. It worked; that was what he told her. We dated: took long walks and built a campfire and watched the sun set over the valley. (Picture of our spot.)

I stayed around the Hale, Barton City, and Glennie areas of Michigan. A couple of good friends of mine from Barton City had been killed in a rollover after bartering over who could take the big turn on the way to Tawas, Michigan, the fastest. One fella called himself the Flying Dutchman. The older man with his kid in the back seat did not survive. For those of you who may remember him as the Flying Dutchman.

When my parents came up to the cabin north of Hale, I introduced my girlfriend to them as the woman I was going to marry. My father treated her as a daughter the rest of his life. My mother didn't like her.

I made my way back to Dearborn Heights, where they had a going-away party for me.

Our spot Our Place - AuSable river MI

Departure from Michigan

I left the next morning for Great Lakes, Illinois, Naval Training Center.

It was a one-day trip that I recall. I checked in, was issued clothes, had a physical, and assigned a company and bunk. I spent two weeks learning naval terminology, then I was put in a prior service company and worked in the mail department for the remaining six weeks before receiving my orders to Norfolk, Virginia, Armed Forces Staff College.

Departure from Great Lakes, Illinois, to Hale, Michigan

I had a transfer leave, so I gave my "to-be wife" an engagement ring to replace the U.S. Army ring I had given her in place of an engagement ring. We started making plans for our wedding.

From there, I went South to catch a flight to Norfolk, Virginia. I checked in and was sent to the barracks at Cent-land-Fleet Command, for barracks duty and some mess cooking, then was assigned to the Armed Forces Staff College maintenance crew. We did cleaning and brightwork and had duty at the theater and library. I was assigned to work with a contractor on the heating and cooling units at the main college building. When that was completed, we installed air-conditioning units in base housing. That worked out so well, I requested a school for air-conditioning.

Chapter 8

MARRIAGE IN MICHIGAN

I REQUESTED LEAVE IN JANUARY of 1965 to get married. The leave was approved, but when it came time to leave, I had to show the chief petty officer that I had the money for a bus ticket. I borrowed the money from my leading petty officer, showed the chief and the chaplain that I had the money, got the leave papers signed, waited till they left, gave the money back, and started hitchhiking to Hale, Michigan.

The trip was slow. It was about 10:00 p.m. when the guy I was riding with got to 94 and 75, southwest of Toledo, Ohio. I was in my dress blues. I walked into a bar, waited till the band took a break, and asked the manager if I could make an announcement. He said I could; so I went on the stage, grabbed the microphone, and asked if anyone was going North. I got to where I was to be at about 2:00 a.m. Saturday.

We got married in the Hale Town Hall at three in the afternoon. It was a community wedding; everyone brought something. We were married by a justice of the peace. The justice of the peace was also a Presbyterian minister. Two weeks later, I let my parents know we were married. My mother was very upset. When my mother demanded to see our marriage license, she noted that the justice of the peace was a minister and signed it "Reverend." She was angry that it was not a priest. She badgered my wife to be a Catholic and be remarried in the Catholic church in Hale.

At one point, the priest threw my wife's Bible at her and told her not to bring it back. On the day of our second wedding, the priest in the confessional booth told my wife the child she was carrying was a bastard. At that remark, my wife reached through the confessional window and slapped the priest on the face. Later in the fall of the same year, my wife went into labor.

October 1965

The Catholic hospital monitored my son but did not do anything to save him. My mother and the hospital were more interested in my son being baptized as a Catholic than saving his life. The loss of my son hurt a great deal, as my wife and I really wanted him. My wife's health condition left me in a difficult situation, as the doctor didn't want her to go back to the environment she had been in. I had to leave to go back to the base, so I arranged for my wife to stay with my younger sister.

After the funeral, I went back to Norfolk, Virginia. Once back at the Armed Forces Staff College, I installed air conditioners in base housing.

Shortly after my return, the navy wanted to show off their latest twin reactor ships and was offering a ride to show it off to the officer students of the college. I overheard the conversation and spoke up as being part of the college maintenance staff. That opened the trip up to us. There were only a few of us from the maintenance crew who went. Within a few days, we were headed out to sea into four-foot waves, which didn't go well with the soldiers. It was my first and last time of being seasick. I was taught how to get over seasickness by one of the ship's crew.

When we came in, I put in for a related school. Shortly after that, a large number of men who had requested the same school changed their minds when a news report (that we would now call fake news) was made public that bad welding caused the ship to sink. Only part of the story was made public, as I learned after I completed the school. I was told I was accepted to the school after I passed the pressure test.

Chapter 9

MORE TRAINING

WHILE WAITING FOR MY ORDERS, I was sent to firefighters training and emergency rescue training, which was part of God's plan to save my wife's right eye. I got my orders for the school and transfer leave. From Norfolk, Virginia, to Groton, Connecticut.

I went to Groton, Connecticut, and checked in for the school; at the same time, the World's Fair was held in New York City, New York. While there, I had shore patrol duty in Groton and in New York City. I did get to go to the World's Fair.

I went to New York City three times while attending school in Connecticut. The classes were hard. We started with about one hundred and sixty students. There were only thirty-seven of us who graduated. After graduation, I got a transfer leave to Charleston, South Carolina.

Another Trip to Michigan

I went back to Michigan for my wife. We said our goodbyes to family and bought a 1960 Ford Country Sedan station wagon with the help of my parents, as they signed for me because I was not old enough to own a car on my own. We went up North to say goodbye to family and friends. We were driving toward Tawas just before the big turn after Iargo Springs when the tie-rod broke, the car went straight, and we crashed into large tree at sixty miles an hour. My wife was driving. She hit her head and got a cut above her right eye. I got a cracked left kneecap. I worked my way to the laundry bag in the back, which had clean clothes in it. I grabbed a pair of underwear, put snow in it, and put it on her eye. The ambulance got there, and as they loaded us, I was told I saved my wife's eye. We were taken to Oscoda Air Force Base. I was given an extended emergency leave.

We were able to get enough from the Ford to buy a 1956 Chevy stick shift. It was hard shifting with a cracked kneecap. We loaded up and left for Charleston, South Carolina. I could only bend my right knee. I had to slide up on the back of the seat to position my foot to put the clutch into shift. We made it there, checked in at the base, and looked for housing. We moved into a small mobile home and checked aboard my assigned ship the following day. I was assigned to the seamen gang until we got under way, then I ran the trash compactor and worked in the laundry room.

My wife settled into our new home and got to know the community and spent time with a ceramic group outside of the trailer park.

From the laundry duty, I had mess cook duty till we returned from my first cruise. When I returned from my first long cruise, I knew what I wanted to do. So, I started studying to be a quartermaster. The ship had a great training instructor. At one point, they had too many quartermasters. I started learning and preparing to work as a quartermaster striker for the next cruise.

We moved out of the trailer park to the first block south of the trailer park. We stayed there till we left for Michigan. While home, before going out to sea again, we purchased a puppy.

The puppy turned out to be a very protective dog against snakes coming near my wife and daughter. On a number of occasions, our dog, Sandy, stopped a snake from getting close to my wife and daughter.

We saw the sights of Charleston Township as we took long walks and learned what there was in the community.

On the next time at sea, I worked in control as a planes man or with the quartermaster on duty. By the time we returned, I had my practical factors signed off and was ready to take the tests for petty officer third-class quartermaster. I took the tests, passed, and was assigned to a ship in Europe.

Chapter 10

THE NEXT BIG MOVE

WE SAID OUR GOODBYES, AND I got my orders from the captain, along with a package to deliver to the other ship. I was given instructions to keep the package close but not to give it special attention. With that and my duffel bag, I was driven to the airport. The plane left Charleston for Washington, DC. Shortly after we reached flight altitude for DC, we started having engine trouble, and three of the four engines failed before we got to DC. We landed on one engine. From there, I flew to New York City. I landed in New York, but at the wrong airport for my next flight. I had no idea how to get there on time. I spoke to a cabdriver and showed him the ticket. He said, "I'll get you there." We were stuck in a traffic jam at Times Square. The driver drove on to the sidewalk to get around the traffic jam. He got me to the other New York airport. I got my stuff checked in, and we departed for Bangor, Maine. Once in the air and leveled off, one of the stewards took five armrests out so I could lie down.

We landed in Ecuador. I ate breakfast and waited for the plane to Madrid, Spain. I had quite a wait for the next scheduled flight, which would have gotten me to Rodda, Spain, after dark. A B-52 that was going to Rodda came in with engine problems. They worked on it for over an hour. I talked to one of the flight crew, to find out if there was room for me. They said there was. They had a problem with taking off, but once in the air, we were okay. We landed at the base, and I checked in at transit. I had changed my rank on all but two uniforms. I was told I was going mess cooking in the morning.

I asked if I could call the watch commander. The reply was that I could not bother him at eight o'clock on a Saturday night. I asked if I could call the ship I was to report to. He said I could. I called and spoke with the captain of the ship. He told me he would send his car for me and wanted to speak to someone at transit for my release. The captain's driver was there in minutes. He took me to the ship. I checked in and gave the package to the skipper. He told me to stow my gear and come down to fire control, and he would show me what I had, how critical the delivery to the ship was.

I'll just say this: I am thankful that I made it without all four engines failing.

Meanwhile, back in the mainland, because I took the B-52, the navy lost track of me and started questioning my wife and others whom I had used as reference for my clearance. We were at sea for two weeks before they stopped the background check. I completed the qualifications necessary for the ship and promotion.

I completed the cruise and transferred to the USS *Hunley* AS-31, a tender in Charleston, South Carolina.

Chapter 11

BACK TO MICHIGAN

THEY WOULD NOT GIVE ME an East Coast older ship, so I told them I would get out.

While on the *Hunley,* I got a job at McDonald's for new tires and traveled back to Michigan. Before being discharged from the U.S. Navy, I did get my GED from Hale High School in Hale, Michigan.

We left Charleston Heights for Michigan. We stopped at my folks to see if we could use their cabin while I looked for a job. I went to work for a construction company as a laborer for bricklayers in Tawas, Michigan.

I worked there till we completed the foundation. When it was completed, I got laid off, until they had another foundation to build.

The employment agency in Tawas was taking applications for the Ford Woodhaven Stamping Plant, in Woodhaven, Michigan. We went South to see if I could work for the Ford stamping plant. I got the job.

A few months after working there, a fella who went by Little John started talking to me about chickens.

I had an interest in metal work and working with steel. I started trade school at Wolverine School of Trades. I took acetylene gas and arc welding. My instructor, Mike Uhons, took an interest in me, as he had served in the navy during WWII and had been a coxswain for General MacArthur. We shared a few sea stories and became friends above teacher and student.

Work was going well at the stamping plant. I got hurt once while working on windshield stone deflectors that hit me in the face.

I took a test to become a foreman but didn't pass because I would not agree that the general foreman was always right.

The stamping plant changed my shift, and I did not want to drop out of trade school. The day I quit Ford's was the same day my wife told me she was pregnant. I looked for another job and told the instructor I was looking for a job. Mike said he would help me find a job where I could work on my welding certification. He told me to apply at Standard Fuel Engineering near the trade school and Delray. The journeyman I was assigned to work for was a pipe fitter welder. I was his "go-for-er." Whatever he needed, I had to go for it. When it came to welding, I literally had to stand on my own welding. I was welding the brackets on industrial ovens. I knew I had to learn other types of welding. I got other welding jobs and continued courses at the trade school.

We bought a house on S. Vanlawn in Westland, Michigan.

A course in heliarc welding got me a job as night shift foreman at Trio Tool & Die Welding Company, in Livonia, Michigan.

I started welding the over-the-street part of streetlight brackets that connect to the pole, which required wire welding. After that, I did heliarc die welding. The day shift foreman quit to start his own business in Flint. I became the night shift foreman. He wanted me to leave Trio and come to work for him in Flint. I worked as the night shift foreman for a while then went to work at Garwood Industries. It was much closer, and the job paid well. I started out as a production line welder then went to working on custom-order trucks. This job put me in a position to see God's Word every day, twice a day: going and coming from work, on the sign next to the road in front of Community Free Will Baptist Church in Westland. Bobby Porter was the pastor then. Back then, preachers would put the main verse of the coming Sunday sermon on both sides of the church sign. So, I got a double dose of Scripture daily.

> For there is one God and one Mediator between God
> and men, the man Christ Jesus. (1 Tim. 2:5 NKJV)

After six days of seeing that Scripture verse twice a day, we went to the Sunday morning service. As stated in the beginning, I accepted Christ as my Savior, and our lives have not been the same since.

Chapter 12

THE ATTACK ON MY WIFE

A FEW WEEKS AFTER I received Christ as my Savior, we were at my parents' home. I was in the basement talking with my father.

I'm not sure what my wife and mother had talked about before they started down the basement steps, my son in her arm and my daughter by the hand. My mother took off her shoe so she could use the heel to hit my wife. I grabbed my mother's arm to stop her from hitting my wife and children.

My father watched it all and said to my mother, "You had that coming."

Things got worse, and we saw them even less as we started looking for the Lord's leading.

The Sale of Our Home

I stayed at Garwood Industries until our home got sold. Because of what I was taught about owing money, we paid off our bills first, when our house sold. The payoff of our home in Westland didn't come till we were in Wisconsin.

The Trip to Wisconsin

The property we went to see in Wisconsin only had one good side looking from the road. The rats had eaten through the area above the basement walls. I asked the realtor what else he had. He took us to Casco.

What else could a young man want? A trout stream at the edge of the property, a lake across the street, the last house in town, three lots away from the school, six lots away from the center of town. We lived on the north side of town, just far enough to watch the Packers on TV. The people on the other side of town could only listen to it on the radio. We got to watch it.

We looked at it and went out on the northwest side of the garden to pray. It was starting to sprinkle. The owner must have thought we were crazy, but he took our offer of our rent being applied to our down payment and then paying him off when our loan went through. He accepted our offer. We moved into the house.

Chapter 13

PREPARING FOR OUR MOVE
TO CASCO, WISCONSIN

WE HAD PURCHASED CHICKENS AND were given rabbits by my elder sister. The kids had outgrown the rabbits, but she didn't want to butcher them, so she gave them to us.

We loaded up our pickup and rented a trailer and took our first load to our new home in Casco. The remaining items and the rabbits would come on the last load.

Going through Chicago at rush hour was hard on the animals, particularly the chickens, as they stopped laying.

We paid our rent toward our down payment and settled in.

I then went looking for a job. We were running out of funds and food. I wanted to have a full tank of gas so I could get back and forth for a week once I got called for a job. We were down to praying for one egg so we could all have pancakes for breakfast, which explains the egg on the front cover of the book. We prayed; God answered. We ate. I walked to the other side of town to see if I could get a job picking apples. The apples needed a week or so. While I was walking back, my wife said that the cannery in Green Bay had called me for an interview. I got a job in the pressure cooker room. The chickens were laying better, and we butchered the older rabbits and considered getting some books on how to produce a rabbit business.

On the next day, I found out a side benefit of working at the cannery was any fruit or vegetable that misses the shoot we could have. So, we had our supply of vegetables all canning season or as long as I worked in the pressure cooker room.

The Good and Bad Sides of Working at the Cannery

The good side was the food, but the bad side was the prisoners who were released for so many hours a day to work at the cannery. My life had started to change for the better after I came to Christ. I was no longer the foulmouthed sailor I had been two years ago because of God's leading and the wise counsel from the Neumanns and the Morgans before leaving Michigan.

So being a Christian among foulmouthed prisoners who would cuss me out and spit at me did not seem like the ideal job, but we had bills to pay.

About the second week, I had about all I could handle. The lead man in the pressure cooker room had been a U.S. Navy middleweight boxing champion. He stood about a foot taller than me. He didn't treat me like the prisoners but just went along with them. I got fed up. I walked in the room attached to the pressure cooker room. He followed me. I was carrying a twelve-inch shim wrench. He walked up to me and looked down. I said, "I am not going to put up with this anymore," as I looked up at him with the shim wrench ready to swing if needed.

He looked down at me and said, "I like you. You got spunk. I won't let the prisoners bother you." He was a man of his word. Shortly after that, a prisoner started calling me names and spitting at me again. The big native picked him up with one arm and held him over the open pressure cooker. He told him, "You do that again and you'll be in it." That was the end of name-calling and spitting.

I didn't know that while I was talking to the lead man, the foreman was watching the happenings and how arguments had stopped. He had seen the talk I had with the lead man (the big Indian) earlier in the day. He motioned for me to come over to his desk. I walked over to his desk. He was looking at my application.

Chapter 14

MY CHANCE FOR A BETTER JOB

HE SAID, "I NOTICED YOU were a welder."

I said, "Yes, but I'm not certified yet."

He told me, "They are begging for welders at the shipyard in Manitowoc. Check it out. Take the test. If it doesn't work out, you still have a job here."

When I got off that afternoon, I gave more thought to what the foreman had said on the drive home. I told my wife what had happened at work that day. We ate supper and prayed about it.

The following Monday, I left for Manitowoc Shipbuilding. I went in and filled out an application. The rest I could fill out after the welding test. I waited over an hour after taking the welding test. The fella giving the test shook my hand and congratulated me. He told me I passed. He asked me how soon I could start. I told him, "Tomorrow."

I found out later that it was the American Ship Certification test.

I started working with a steel fitter, tacking the pipes in place on forty-foot booms, and welding the connectors on the ends. I did cutting and learned to use a carbon arc. The fitter had me get into a steel basket and had the overhead crane operator pick me up about twenty feet to weld a crane boom, I guess, to see if I could handle working out of a raised basket. After being a lineman, that was easy.

Back at the homestead, we were looking into better ways to produce rabbits and eggs. In the process, I found two grocery stores that tried our fresh processed rabbit meat that passed the meat inspection. The second month, they wanted all we could bring them.

Shortly after this, they closed on our former house back in Westland. We went to the bank, but the only local credit we had was at the feed mill. We were able to get a loan for the farmstead and pay off the former owners.

The village was small but friendly except for the priest at the local Catholic church who looked at our last name and demanded we pay the fall drive. I told him we were not Catholic, and we were not paying it. My evenings of kneeling in the mud in my aunt's garden with my relatives to say the rosary were over.

We got to know some of our neighbors. One of them across the road a half mile north was an apple and pig farmer. He asked me to help him castrate his male pigs. I did, and he gave me one. He told me the pig had a stomach problem and that we had to butcher it at about seventy pounds. We placed the pig in a pen under two apple trees. We found the pig running down the street being chased by a group of kids. The kid who caught it said it was his. I said, "I don't think so," and took the pig. I put it back in its pen and made sure it couldn't get out. A few weeks after that, the pig was getting pretty close to seventy pounds. Because one of my relatives got bitten by a pig when I was much younger on the farm, I was somewhat fearful of pigs. I opened the pig's pen and lassoed it. That worked till the pig saw the corn we had in our garden on to the way car. I stopped and had my wife hold the rope, while I got a feed bag. I got the pig's attention with a cob of sweet corn and threw it in the feed bag. It worked. I took the pig to the butcher shop. I picked up our processed pig the next day.

While living in Casco, I joined the Naval Reserve unit in Green Bay; which would be a fallback employment position in the future.

My wife caused some resentment because she started a clothing alteration business.

I did some repair welding on a neighbor's farm equipment. He was well pleased. However, the same people who complained about the rabbits, chickens, and my wife's business wanted me to open a welding shop.

Prayer Can Change Habits

I had quit smoking. I didn't think it made sense to be in smoke all day and have a cigarette on break. I chewed tobacco. I had prayed about quitting. I ran out of tobacco. We went up to Algoma to go trout fishing and let the kids play in the park. I prayed about quitting chewing tobacco. I told my wife I was going to buy some chew. As I turned to walk back to the truck, a man walked up and said, "Here," and gave me a big bag of potato chips. He said, "For you and your family." I thanked him. And thanked the Lord for His answer. That was the end of chewing tobacco for me.

We went to Green Bay to see what it had for churches. We found one that was like the one we had gone to with the Neumanns and Morgans. We started attending regularly, and I realized I had known the pastor and his wife years before when I worked as a jumper for the Detroit Free Press. They had worked at Ford Motor Company in Livonia, Michigan, before his call to the ministry. We were baptized and joined the church and attended regularly.

Chapter 15

THE CALL TO SERVICE

SHORTLY AFTER BECOMING MEMBERS OF the church, I was on my knees cutting the bands on a bundle of eight-foot-long pipes when I heard my name. I looked up and asked, "Soyer, what do you want?"

He replied, "I didn't say anything."

I put my helmet down and heard "Pat." I lifted my helmet again and said, "What?"

He answered, "I didn't say anything."

I put my helmet down and remembered Samuel in the Scriptures had to be called three times. I said, "Yes, Lord, what do you want me to do?"

The Lord answered me. He said, "You to go to the hospital in Algoma."

I went back to cutting the steel bands around the pipes for the crane beams.

I went home and told my wife, "We need to pray about something. I told her what happened at work. She knew my feelings about hospitals and medical centers.

I had such a fear of them that before I was married, I would hold my breath until I drove past it. The reason for this fear was a terrible sore my father got on his arm from being near or at a medical clinic on his way to work, while waiting for the bus.

We prayed about it. After the Sunday services, after we came home, I went to the hospital in Algoma. I walked down the hallways till God let me know which room to go into. I went in and read the

Scripture to a ninety-eight-year-old woman, a retired schoolteacher whom people of the community had been praying for. I had prayer with her and left. I still remember her last name then, but I'm sure she's passed on.

After that, I called more often. I remember a call I made shortly before a bad winter storm was already hitting southern Wisconsin and I was about an hour away by the time I left the hospital. I walked the halls as I had done before. The Lord said, "Here." There was a teenage girl, about fifteen, whose parents were called by the nurses to tell them she wouldn't make it till morning. I went in and spoke to her. She was in a bad way. I called out to God to heal her and restore her. I left the hospital to make it home before the snowstorm.

My wife and I called her at their home a month later. Her mother asked, "What did you do? They said she would be dead by morning." We didn't hear that she recovered till after the storm. Her recovery had greater impact on the community than we knew. Many years later in Rochester, Minnesota, the Brethren pastor from the church west of Casco told me there was a revival in that part of the state of Wisconsin.

> Who hath saved us, and called us with an holy calling, not according to our works, but according to his own purpose and grace, which was given us in Christ Jesus before the world began. (2 Tim. 1:9)

That was the beginning of my calling ministry, which I didn't know what that was till the deacon board at Fourth Baptist appointed me as a shut-in calling pastor.

Chapter 16

THE IMPACT OF A RADIO MINISTRY

Pacific Garden Mission

AT THE TIME I STARTED calling at the hospital, we began listening to a program called Pacific Garden Mission. The director would often talk about the name of the church Calvary. If someone wanted to go to the bar at the end of the dead end street, that is called the Gates of Hell. He would often say, "You have to pass Calvary to reach the Gates of Hell. We all have that choice."

Two college-age young men in the next town called into the radio station about accepting Christ. They did. The preacher told them to find a non liturgical church to attend. The only one around was a Brethren Church, west of us a few miles, that our pastor in Green Bay told us to go to if we couldn't get to Green Bay.

They went there, joined the church, and impacted the whole area for the Lord.

Back at the shipyard, things were going great. They moved me to different sections of the shop to work different parts of the cranes. It was challenging as one day I'd be welding steel a quarter inch thick, the next day a four-inch-thick steel deck. After working in the different departments, I must have got their attention, as they offered me a position on the assembly of cranes team that goes to wherever the crane is being sent. It would mean from the time I got the call,

I had so many hours to get to the airport. I didn't turn them down, but I told those offering the position I would have to talk it over with my wife. We needed to pray about it. After we prayed about it, we decided that I would turn down their offer, because it was not what God had planned for me to do.

I continued my calling ministry and had a Bible study in Algoma.

There was also a new church starting north of Manitowoc. The services were being held in an American Legion Hall. It was where I preached my first sermon.

Our other pastor back at the Green Bay Church told me we should pray about going to the Bible college in Watertown. We prayed about it.

Another Move

I was able to find an apartment to rent and got a job at Watertown Metals. I started out working on snowmobiles then got put in their maintenance department. We sold our farmstead in the spring of 1971.

I went down and enrolled and looked for work before we put our house up for sale.

I continued the ministry I was called to do earlier in the book.

Chapter 17

THE CALL TO SERVICE

WHEN I CAME TO CHRIST, I was unchurched, not a member of any church, until we joined the Green Bay Baptist Church, in Green Bay, Wisconsin.

My First Sermon

There was also a new church north of Manitowoc, which was started by one of the students from the Bible college in Watertown. The services were being held in an American Legion Hall. It was where I preached my first sermon. (picture)

After preaching that first time, I got assurance from God that I could do this with His help. This was the beginning of many years of praying, hospital calling, and preaching.

Our other pastor back at the Green Bay Church told me we should pray about going to the Bible college in Watertown. We prayed about it and checked it out.

I preached my first sermon First Preaching

I will instruct you and teach you in the way you
should go; I will guide you with My eye. (Ps.32:8)

I continued to work at the shipyard until the next semester started. I gave notice that I was leaving my job at Manitowoc
Shipbuilding. The opportunities I had with that job would have
included world travel and very good pay. In the welding profession,
I had reached the top at that time, but that was not God's plan for
me at that time. Much of what I had learned from the training at the
shipyard helped me perfect what I had learned in Wolverine School
of Trades, which would also help with setting up a contract welding
business at a later date, while I was in the seminary in Minneapolis,
Minnesota.

From Crane Building to Church Building

I went to enroll in the early fall of 1970. I was able to find an apartment to rent and got a job at Watertown Metals. I started out working on snowmobiles then got put in their maintenance department

working with a Bible college student who was older and a licensed electrician, Bill H. He was a unique fella to work with. He had gotten pyrexia and lost many of his teeth while he was serving in the U.S. Navy. He loved to sing an old church hymn called "In the Garden" every day as he walked into the maintenance room, as only Bill could sing it without teeth.

I took a few courses in the mornings to get an understanding of the college lifestyle. I was not impressed. I felt somewhat uncomfortable because of the age difference and my life experiences before coming to a college community.

We worked out an agreement on our farmstead, the same way we had purchased it when we bought it: rent with the option to buy. We closed on the sale of it in the spring of 1971.

Farmstead - Looking from the bridge

Farmstead Northside of the house

Farmstead - Casco

Farmstead on Casio Green House porch

With much prayer, I continued taking more Bible college courses in the fall of 1971. There was a fairly large age gap between me and most of the other students, as many of them were right out of high school, home school, or Christian day school.

Bible College

Things were better once my wife and children came down to Watertown.

We joined a local church in Watertown. When the college spring semester had ended, we worked with a pastor who started a new church in Green Bay, Wisconsin. Somehow the pastor worked it out for us to live in the old Green Bay Packers training camp for part of the summer. I worked with the pastor, calling and inviting families out to church in the neighborhood near the church. We spent over a month in the camp on the shore of Lake Michigan. After the church planting work in Green Bay, we went to Watertown and got back into college.

GBP (Green Bay Packer) Bunk Cabin camp

GBP Camp Now

GBP Camp Now

GBP Camp Now - Lake Side View

GBP Shower Room

While at the college and the local church in Watertown, we listened to a number of missionary speakers. We talked about it, prayed, and asked God for His leading and guidance in the matter of mission work. We prayed about serving the Lord on an Indian reservation in the Northwest Territories of Canada. We accepted the call to serve as missionaries in the Northwest Territories of Canada to the Native Americans there. We were accepted and approved by Baptist Mid-Missions.

Apartment Complex in Watertown WI

Our renters bought our farmstead back in Casco. We closed on the farmstead and moved the rest of our belongings to Watertown and rented a storage room for what we didn't need in the apartment we rented. We moved into the apartment complex on the northeast side of Watertown across from the cemetery. While working at Watertown Metals, I was offered a very large old-fashioned toolbox. I accepted the offer. It was too big to put in a car, and we no longer had our truck. I used a steel cart to pull it home. I physically pulled it home. Because it was shorter to take the road through the cemetery, that was what I did. Shortly after I got to the apartment, the police were in the cemetery, because someone had said there were grave robbers in the cemetery. I guess the sound of steel wheels on a hard stone road at night sounds spooky.

Cemetery Gate Across from Apartment

I was still in the Naval Reserve in Green Bay, so I transferred to the Madison, Wisconsin, unit. I had a number of classes and was assigned to doing recruitment for operations in Vietnam. I showed movies and talked about the operations and training opportunities to serve there. While in a phone booth, just before leaving for Washington, I gave a guy in our unit a track about how to become a Christian. He took it. By the time of the meeting the following month, he told me he had accepted Christ as his Savior and joined the local church of his girlfriend and attended there, and they were making plans for their coming wedding.

Chapter 18

THE SENN LETTER

BECAUSE WE HAD GIVEN EVERYTHING to the Lord in the move to Casco, we continued to open our home to missionaries who couldn't go home because home was too far. We opened our home to two missionaries during a holiday weekend. My wife and I were having a discussion about a letter from her sister. One of the two missionaries thought we were talking about a letter known as the Senn Letter.

The letter, which we had heard about, was about an embezzlement having to do with the founder of a Bible college and another founder of a different Bible college that was started, but I had not read it, until after I was expelled from the Bible college I was attending for reading it. After the holiday, the missionary went to the founder and president of the college and told him we had read the Senn Letter. He called me to inform me that I was expelled for reading the Senn Letter. I told him there is no law that says it's against the law to read a letter! We did read the letter then. I was not about to let this arrogant college president cause me to lose my GI Bill for his ego.

I felt betrayed by this missionary we had opened our home to.

(Another picture of the college)

When wisdom enters your heart, and knowledge is pleasant to your soul,

Discretion will preserve you; Understanding will keep you,

To deliver you from the way of evil, From the man who speaks perverse things,

From those who leave the paths of uprightness to walk in the ways of darkness. (Prov. 2: 10-13)

I got a lawyer. He worked on it, and we won. I asked him what I owed him. He said, "Pay me when you get to Fat City!"
I said, "I pay my debts! What do I owe you?"
He said, "Thirty-six dollars!" I paid him.

Chapter 19

CHANGE OF DIRECTIONS

I WENT TO THE NAVAL Reserve Center to let them know what our intentions were, so far as going to the mission field in the Northwest Territories of Canada. I was told, "You can go, but not your wife and children, or your wife and children can go but not you, because of your previous duties." The Vietnam War was still on, and some of the protesters were living in the Northwest Territories of Canada.

So we prayed about the situation. I went back to the Naval Reserve Center and told them I wanted to go back on active duty. Shortly after, in about a week, I got orders for active duty in Hawaii. We had time, so we drove, camping in parks all the way to San Francisco, California. I checked in. The first thing I was asked was "Why did you bring your family?"

Evidently the navy had no intentions of putting me on a ship. They wanted me to do the same type of work I had done in Kentucky, Illinois, Virginia, Spain, and South Carolina. They offered me duty with the military police that would have put my family in danger. I turned them down, as this was something I knew much more about than they knew. One of the main reasons I wanted to get away from gangs and organized crime and all that goes with it in Detroit and Dearborn Heights, Michigan. One of the things that makes certain persons have natural abilities without having special training as they have seen criminal situations from the inside. They know how to watch and not be noticed but know what they have seen. The higher-ups in criminal organizations back then knew how to check

58

the backgrounds of those they think might be working undercover against them, but if there are no records of schooling for that, there was no way to know for sure. I don't know if the higher-ups thought I had that ability, but I knew of the dangers my family would be in. I knew more about street crimes, prostitution, human trafficking, and drugs than they knew.

Chapter 20

CALIFORNIA TO HAWAII

I WAS TRANSFERRED TO THE ship pictured in Seawolf Park in Texas.

The ship was then operating out of Pearl Harbor, Hawaii. I checked into transit, got housing for my family, and checked aboard the ship.

Picture of the ship

My brother & I at Seawolf Park, Texas

While still getting settled in, we went for a walk in the woods in the back of the fourplex we lived in. There were a number of fruit trees there: dates, bananas, and coconut trees.

My vagueness about locations and ships is explained by the picture taken of the remains of my former ship at Seawolf Park on Galveston Island, Texas. For those of you who are navy veterans, I'm sure you understand.

RAFT Training

We had some ops in the Hawaii area, then I was told I was going to be a Race Relation Facilitator Training (RAFT). Another shipmate and I spent one week of fourteen-hour classroom days to complete our RAFT training and certification. RAFT training involved a way to deal with the racial problems in the country and in the military. Tradmons, cultures, and colors were all dealt with. My partner from the sub at Seawolf Park on Galveston Island, Texas, was Hispanic, which was the normal partnership of two different races for the same duty station or ship. Within two weeks, we had our first racial problem to deal with. We submitted a verbal report to the XO and the captain of the ship. If that didn't stop the problem, we could go to the base commander. The remarks being made were more of envy and jealousy of a black man who was born on a plantation in Louisiana and was a top-notch sailor with a beautiful Korean wife. They would make remarks that everyone should own one like him. He was the type of sailor who was always a top achiever. He was always at the top of any test for advancement. He was a man who would take a college course rather than watch movies when we were at sea.

to Race Relation Training School to correct the attitude of separation the Bible college founder was insinuating to the students of the college. According to the founder of the Bible college, persons of other colors or cultures should stay with their own kind. There should be a separation.

Where I grew up, in Detroit, I had friends of many colors and cultures because of the cultures of the neighborhoods: German, Polish, Jewish, French, Italian, along with other areas of eastern European neighborhoods, and the blacks and Orientals who came to Noble Elementary School from Fort Wayne, in downtown Detroit, Michigan.

After RAFT Training

We set out for some longer cruises, most near the islands, then over toward Northern California and Washington and north of Seattle. I did happen to be on military police duty near Vancouver in Nanaimo when a very famous actor was arrested for drugs and sexual assault in the midseventies and was found guilty again today: April 26, 2018.

Back in Hawaii, things were going good for my wife and children.

While I was out to sea, my wife found a Christian day school and got the kids enrolled. The children loved it. We got involved with their building projects for a larger school and the servicemen's center and outreach program, which included training and street preaching on the strip in Honolulu.

Hawaii - China mans Hat a very small island off the east side of Hawaii

Hawaii - Our friends lived at the bottom of Coco Head Mountain

Hawaii - Pat and son

Hawaii - Pat in HI

Hawaii - Pearl Harbor where Pat was stationed out of

Hawaii - Spacecapel landing in Hawaii

Hawaii - The Arizona Memorial in Pearl Harbor

Our longest cruise while I was on that ship was north of Point Barrow, Alaska.

The ship had been partly flooded twice and had not been in port long enough to clean the mildew and stop it from growing in the bilges of the ship.

When we were in port in Hawaii, I was sent to the hospital for a medical exam to try to figure out what I was allergic to. After a number of tests and patches on my back for a week or so, I was told I was allergic to mildew and Johnsongrass, which grows around many of the shipyards and lakes all over the world. If the ship had stayed in port long enough to clean the ship, it would have cleaned the mildew out of the bilges. I could have avoided the Johnsongrass once I knew what it looked like. But I was transferred back to transit.

Chapter 21

A CHANGE OF DUTY

WHILE IN TRANSIT, I OVERSAW work parties on base maintenance and other jobs on and off the base. (Pictures of school & Church 10 & 11) look up pictures of Koolau Baptist) call Hawaii

On my time off, I worked on the Christian day school expansion using some light equipment for moving dirt and gravel and the servicemen's center of the church, which included a street ministry on the strip in Honolulu.

The pastor of the servicemen's center outreach told me he graduated from Central Seminary and that I should check it out. That gave us a destination to think about in the future. We felt at that time that God was leading us to work as missionaries to the Native American reservation near Ashland, Wisconsin.

Our future was somewhat uncertain. We prayed about it. I got orders to a ship. My official job title was a quartermaster, an old fashioned quartermaster who trains so if need be, he can take command of the ship. I was on the ship for about a week. We set out to sea just a few hundred yards from the same channel I had been going through for months, when we stopped. The captain said he was informed that the admiral wanted our ship to be facing north. I checked our position and told him I would check the depth. I had been in and out of that channel a number of times, and I knew there was a sandbar there, but the draft on the last ship I was on was so much less we didn't have to worry about it. I knew the sandbar was there. I checked the sea level above the sandbar. I told him there was a large sandbar that our rudder would get stuck in. The last ship I was on didn't have the same draft below the waterline, and we stayed clear of the sandbar by staying in the channel. He gave the order to the helmsman and the engine room. We got stuck. While we were waiting for the tugboats to pull us off the sandbar, I said two words: "Told ya." He had me transferred back to transit the next day. Transit told me that they would like to transfer me to a Marine Corps base near Calico, California, doing the same off-base work I was doing in Hawaii. I said no.

My off-base jobs varied from making deliveries to doing shore patrol duty or just being in the right place at the right time to get information on people or situations of interest to the military. That worked out for a while, but I'm not a big fan of organized crime. I knew what I was doing, and the more successful I was at getting information on criminal activity, the more danger I was putting myself and wife and children were in.

Koolau Baptist Church where Pat learned to Street Preach

Koolau - Church

Koolau Baptist Church in Hawaii

Chapter 22

ANOTHER BIG MOVE

SO I ASKED THOSE ABOVE me in the chain of command if I could be transferred to Great Lakes, Illinois, and to be discharged from there. They gave me what I asked for, and I went to housing to arrange for our household furnishings and appliances to go to Superior, Wisconsin, then to transportation to get our car shipped to California. We were so surprised by how many of our neighbors came over to help us with cleaning for the final inspection before leaving Hawaii.

While in the airport, we purchased vine-ripened pineapples at a very low price. We used that pineapple box to get our dog in and out past the front desk. We had to wait two days for our car to reach California and get processed in.

When our car was released to us, we loaded up our traveling luggage, kids, and dog and headed east for Green Bay, Wisconsin. Once we got to Pastor Don Dehl's, I told them what our plans were, to wait for the paperwork on my discharge to be completed in Great Lakes, Illinois. Then we would pick up my discharge papers and go to Michigan. Before leaving, he also told me to check out Central Seminary. I told him I would.

We left our kids with the Dehls while we went to Great Lakes, got my papers, and went back for the kids. We checked with our families in Michigan.

They wanted us to come and visit while we waited for our household items to arrive in Superior, Wisconsin.

Chapter 23

BACK TO MICHIGAN

WE WENT TO MICHIGAN AND saw our families in the Detroit and Hale areas. Then we went to Minneapolis to check out Central Seminary.

We did, prayed about it, and stayed with a Christian family we met at the seminary. We rented their house and purchased it the following year.

God answered our prayers. We worked out our traveling expenses, having our household items moved from Superior, Wisconsin, to Minneapolis, Minnesota, and enough funds to put a down payment on the triplex we had stayed in two blocks from Central Seminary. We paid rent until we closed on the house. I looked for a job and found one in Bloomington, south of Minneapolis.

I worked afternoons, which worked out well as I enrolled at Central Seminary part-time. We enrolled our children in the Christian day school connected with the church and seminary and joined the church. After my first part-time semester, I was asked to come before the deacon board about being licensed to marry and burry and be a shut-in calling pastor, under the other calling pastor. I accepted it. It was a voluntary position, but it was what God called me to do. One of the families I called on had a daughter who was in a wheelchair and had some of the other health issues that come with limited use of limbs. We would face the same situation when my daughter got into an accident.

Triplex - Remodeled Room

Triplex - Another Picture

Triplex in MPLS MIN

One of the most memorable moments of Talley was how she liked to tell hurting people about Jesus. I went to call on her in a hospital in Minneapolis. She had spoken to a young man in his late teens or early twenties with a broken spine about where he would spend eternity. He had gone swimming and decided to jump off a rather high bridge and hit the cement pillar at the bottom next to the river. Talley had gone to him through an area that was undergoing reconstruction. She was quite determined to make it through the construction area in a wheelchair. She talked to this young man and told him she would send the calling pastor to see him. I spoke with him about his need to accept God's Son, Jesus Christ, as his Savior from sin and spend eternity in heaven. Talley let me know that the young man died four hours after I left.

An Addition to Calling

I started doing services in some of the hospitals and nursing homes on a regular basis. My daughter would come along and play her trumpet with the hymns.

I started going to seminary full-time, even if I was still working full-time in Bloomington. The church asked me to accept a deacon position. I accepted it. As a deacon at Fourth Baptist Church, I was assigned a number of families to call on and pray for and encourage as part of my responsibilities of being a deacon. By the time I graduated, I had worked as a youth leader, Sunday school teacher, shut-in and nursing home preacher, camp counselor, Christian day school bus driver, and pulpit supply preacher in a four-state area.

Things were coming together in the seminary as well as the welding shop I worked at in Bloomington. I got promoted from spot welding to pressure tank welding with a very reasonable raise in pay.

I developed a calling ministry to the shut-ins at home, hospitals, and nursing homes. The outreach to shut-ins, hospitals, and nursing homes was a very important outreach of Fourth Baptist Church.

My wife and I both took courses at the University of Minnesota. Most were about the Native Americans in Michigan, Wisconsin, and Minnesota, and American Short Story so I would have the needed credits for a four-year degree. My wife graduated from Fourth Baptist Bible Institute in 1980. She also worked as a supervisor at Fashion Fit Tailors. About this same time, the company I worked for wanted me to become their day shift welding department foreman, because they were no longer going to have an afternoon shift. The company wanted me to drop out of seminary. I said no, because I didn't think that was God's will for me at that time.

Chapter 24

IF YOU DON'T HAVE
A JOB, MAKE ONE

I STARTED DOING LANDSCAPING AND contract welding, which in most cases more than replaced the income from the welding shop. Because I was not prejudiced, I wasn't afraid to look for customers in the same neighborhood I was taking courses at night. I worked out a deal on lawn care, tree removal, and putting in a fenced parking lot. The customer I worked for was employed by Urban Renewal. He was well satisfied and referred me to other customers in Saint Paul as well as gave me a good reference to others in the neighborhood.

> Whatever your hand finds to do, do it with your might; for there is no work or device or knowledge or wisdom in the grave where you are going. (Eccles. 9:10)

Welding picked up also. I repaired dumpsters for a solid waste company. The owner of the company came up with an idea that he was going to have his wife, a Minneapolis City official employee, submit it to the city council to require garbage cans to be put in a rack so many inches off the ground to control mice and rats. He had a design for a garbage can rack. Shortly after that, I was offered a partnership with the owner to run the production of the racks if his wife could get it passed by the city council. There were too many other things that were going on there that the police department were overlooking because of his wife's position with the city. I told him, "Not at this time." The truth was that I didn't want my name on something with him as an owner because of the other things that were going on there. The man kept a gun on his desktop. I asked him what the gun was for. He said, "It solves arguments." That was enough for me.

Chapter 25

GOD HAD A PLAN AND ANOTHER DIRECTION FOR ME

SHORTLY AFTER THAT, I WENT into another phase in my training as a pulpit supply preacher mainly in Minnesota, Wisconsin, and a few times in North and South Dakota.

I completed the courses I was taking at the University of Minnesota on Native American Indians in Michigan, Wisconsin, and Minnesota and the course American Short Story so I could graduate in 1981. As the final semester was starting, we started making plans for the graduation party. I invited my parents to the graduation. They came, my mother with some resentment. They came to the party, disappointed that it was alcohol free (not their style), but well wishing.

After the party, they left the next day.

After everything went back to normal, I continued being a pulpit supply preacher in Minnesota, Wisconsin, and North Dakota. I was sent to Flom, Minnesota, and soon after preached in Mentor and accepted the position I was offered as pastor. We moved to Mentor into the parsonage. I pastored the church there for about eight months or so. I was getting complaints for not having confirmation classes. Baptists don't have confirmation classes. I resigned. We moved to a farmstead near Eldred, Minnesota. I had started working for the Crookston School District shortly after accepting the church in Mentor.

I continued working for the school district in Crookston. We started an egg business on the farmstead near Eldred, which worked out very well.

My family was doing well. My wife had a good job, and our children were involved with 4-H, which worked out well with the chickens and rabbits.

Working for the school district worked out very well; I also drove a regular school route, plus sports events. I also worked on the school buses and some of the school district's maintenance equipment. That worked out really well also. I continued being a pulpit supply preacher for churches in Minnesota and North Dakota.

I was wondering why our triplex in Minneapolis was not getting sold. So I took some real estate courses at the University of Minnesota in Crookston to see what I could do to get our former home sold in Minneapolis.

In the process of taking the courses in real estate, I came across a person who said if I take one more course and pass the state test, I could work for a real estate broker in Crookston. By the time I finished that one more course, our former house in Minneapolis had been sold. We paid some bills and saved the rest while we waited on the Lord. We were active in a local church in a nearby town.

Working in real estate seemed to be working well for me, and my wife's job for the intercounty Community Council seemed to be working well also.

I considered buying a real estate franchise. We didn't pray it through as we had when we left Wisconsin. We should have prayed it through before purchasing a real estate. We didn't and were not ready for the coming tragedy of our daughter's car accident.

> Wait on the LORD; Be of good courage, And He shall strengthen your heart; Wait, I say, on the LORD! (Ps. 27:14 NKJV)

Chapter 26

THE ACCIDENT

MY SON WAS STILL IN high school. My daughter was in college, living in the college dorm at a university in Crookston. As a friend was driving with his buddy in the front seat, my daughter and another girl were in the back seat on the way back to the college dorm. The driver suffered from heart failure and died while he was driving. His buddy in the front passenger seat grabbed the steering wheel to keep the car from going off the road into the muddy field, turned the steering wheel too sharply, and caused the car to roll over four times, injuring my daughter and the other young woman in the back seat. The other passengers were hurt, but not as bad as the two women.

My daughter had a broken neck that left her without the use of her legs and limited use of her arms. The students in the front seat had cuts and bruises. The other student in the back seat with my daughter had internal injuries as well.

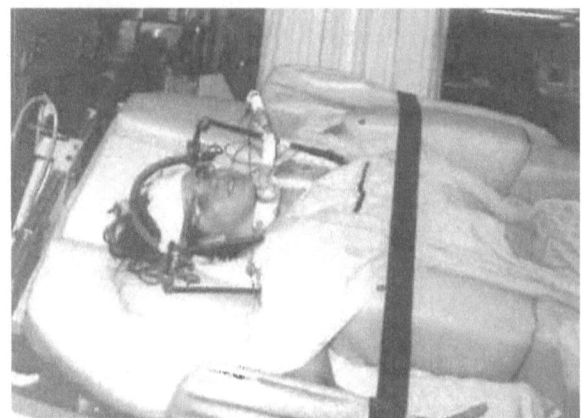

Accident - Hospital Bed

Accident - Car Wreck

The real estate company I purchased gave us two years of heartache and financial worries. In the process, I got into health and life insurance while continuing to be a pulpit supply preacher and working my way out of the real estate company I had purchased. We then purchased a large lot to have a house built for us to live in on the ridge about eight miles east of town. I ran my real estate and insurance businesses out of our home/office, until a week before my daughter 's wedding.

Front of House (Now)

I also started an additional clothing business called Plus Enterprises. That worked for a while, but not enough to have Independence Plus and the power to print clothing in the same building. We built another building in the back so I could make scarfs, beadwork, leather goods, and printed clothing for powwows, as I was a licensed vendor.

Chapter 27

BACK IN THE MILITARY

I JOINED THE LOCAL ARMY National Guard unit in Crookston. I had been out of the Naval Reserve for more than four years, so a lot of the training was reorienting me from navy to army. The opposite of when I went from the Michigan Army National Guard to the navy when I was seventeen. I trained in a number of areas the first year. After that, I did some ops away from Crookston, in Minnesota, North Dakota, South Dakota, California, Wisconsin, and Canada, with the Canadian military. I was training in North Dakota, with the Dakota Guard, when they got assigned flood duty. I worked on the sandbag team near the flooding Red River of the North in Grand Forks, North Dakota. I think I did a good job as I was one of the group members the governor personally thanked at a photo shoot with the governor of North Dakota in Grand Forks at a meeting after the flood.

After the flood, I was sent to a number of schools covering a number of different subjects of security, desert survival, rappelling, winter survival, and a course that taught us how to do the most damage to the enemy with the least risk. I was put in a strike unit in another town. That would put me in another country in forty-eight hours, if needed. Things kind of mellowed out after a couple years, but the unit had more plans for me. I was concerned about being activated for another war.

A Double Motive for the Move

One of the insurance companies I sold insurance for had a supervisor position opening in Duluth. I considered the position but wanted to check out Duluth. I checked the guard unit there. The type of unit was called light equipment maintenance. That sounded safer to me than combat support or the units I was connected to in Crookston and Moorehead.

As things were heating up in the Middle East, I looked closer at the unit in Duluth, Minnesota, and transferred to it. We should have prayed about it more. What do you think light equipment maintenance would mean? To me, that sounded safe. However, it was the first unit activated in Minnesota. It was redesignated as combat support.

The unit was activated about six months after I transferred to the Duluth unit.

The unit back in Crookston and the strike unit in the other town didn't get activated for the Gulf Conflict.

Chapter 28

SEPTEMBER 11, 1990

WE WERE BRIEFED ON VARIOUS things to expect once we were in country. We went to transit then to the Expo Center. Before leaving the Expo Center, I was asked to take a course on counseling wounded service people. I was told they were expecting one hundred thousand casualties. I was told I would get a commission as a chaplain. The expectation of one hundred thousand casualties was not the news I wanted to hear.

To be a commissioned chaplain was a good thing, but not for a hundred thousand casualties. I am thankful we didn't have the casualties they were expecting.

The stress brought out the best and worst in a number of unit members. At this point, the worst was yet to come. Most of the unit was assigned to work at the air base on mail and equipment being shipped in until the Scud attacks started. Then the other end of the base was being attacked by a ground force, and things got crazy. During the Scud attacks, there were a number of people in the unit who lost it. The forces on the other side of the base were able to stop the enemy ground forces before they could damage the aircraft on that side of the base. That was a scary time, as we didn't have the firepower to do much if they got through the other side of the base where we were handling the incoming mail.

From there, we were sent to Camp Rambo, where we were also under Scud attacks. We left there to the north to Camp Welsh. We had moved further northeast toward the oil fields. By the time of the cease-fire, the oil fields had been burning for days. The unit was southeast of the oil field fires near the end of the conflict, as it was designated by the federal government and the Veterans of Foreign Wars. Not a war. We went back for processing back to the States. Once we were back in Duluth, we had a lot of unpacking to do with equipment as well as our own personal gear. The next week was pretty busy, then things went back to somewhat normal as we learned our unit would be phased out at a later date and reestablished in a Southern state.

Many of the members of the unit including myself have disabilities to deal with the rest of our lives: post-traumatic stress, the chemicals from the Scuds, and the fumes from the burning oil fields. It has been more than twenty years, and I am still treating the rash of two different kinds. The one doctor I had at the veterans clinic in Fargo had been in the same area as our unit. He was dealing with the same rash as I have. He told me how to control it but told me I would have it the rest of my life. He passed about five years ago. The other rash was clearly diagnosed about two years ago. The rash has improved, but I am still treating it. The other things I just have to live with.

I was discharged and released from the Minnesota National Guard.

Chapter 29

BACK TO DAKOTA FELLOWSHIP

I WENT TO WORK FOR Dakota Fellowship, which involves Bible studies, preaching, and church planting. I was still a pulpit supply preacher and worked at three churches: two in Minnesota and one in North Dakota.

The pastor and his family had come out to the farmstead near Eldred, where we were living before I was activated by the guard unit in Duluth. His church was located near the air force base in North Dakota. He had wanted me to candidate at his church, as he knew he was being transferred.

I was spread too thin by the time I came back from the Gulf Conflict. I was working with three groups before his transfer. The largest of the three was the church in Emerado, North Dakota. (Picture from I phone of the church)

While I was doing that, I was also a chaplain for the Grand Forks Civil Air Patrol.

The other two were in Minnesota, one outside of Crookston, the other about seventy miles north of Crookston. Almost all of that church was connected to one family and a few neighbors who lived near where we met.

A bad car accident, a heart attack, and the flood of '97 pretty much sent part of that congregation back to Texas.

The church in Emerado called a pastor from the air base. I continued preaching and holding Bible studies in the Crookston area. We became a registered church in our township with about eight to twelve regular attendees.

We have had our ups and downs over the years. One of the ups was a guest who wrote the program for *Purpose-Driven Life for Youth* and the movie. We were full to the point of standing room only. If you haven't seen the movie, you might want to if you can find it. Over the years, we have continued to have Christian movies and vacation Bible time when we have the kids again. At present, I'm still pastoring, calling, and writing. Our church has had its ups and downs, as we wait for His return.

It is my hope that this book will help the readers come to a personal relationship with Christ and seek God's will and plan for their life.

I will close this with a poem from jacksbrandbooks.com: "The Heart of a Good Man."

The heart of a good man has his faith in a better man—one that's divine and with him all the time.

> The heart of the better man always understands—always lends a guiding hand—even when the good man doesn't understand. The trust is still there—he can always share with the Divine Man that cares.
>
> The heart of a good man has an inner joy that this world can't shake, break, or destroy. Though the world says he's wrong, in his heart there's a song.
>
> The world's fame and fashions are not his attractions.
>
> A "Well done, my faithful servant" is his goal, and on this he'll bet his soul, his fortune, and his eternity.

Additional Photo Gallery

774 Van Lawn, Ml

Van Lawn, Ml - 2018

Pat in uniform

Estate (entrance)

1970

My Father Wife and Children and Me

Neumanns - My Wife and I with the Neumanns at ARK Encounter in Kentucky

Presidential Inauguration - Capitol

Presidential Inauguration - Capitol

Presidential Inauguration - Gathering at the temple before

Presidential Inauguration Meeting

Presidential Inauguration - Inauguration Meeting at the Temple

Presidential Inauguration - Photo of inside the former black Jewish Temple

Presidential Inauguration with the Presidential Look-alike

Presidential Inauguration • Temple

Presidential Inauguration

Pat Baranski

www.ingramcontent.com/pod-product-compliance
Lightning Source LLC
Chambersburg PA
CBHW020321130626
46549CB00003B/959